# *"The Power to Prosper"* - Rob Voorhees

*Whether the economy is right-side up, upside down, or stuck sideways, your ability to prosper is "out of this world" anyway! There is a tsunami of wealth coming to the people of God, trillions of dollars as a matter of fact. God wants us to get ready to receive it and know what to do with it once we get it.*

## Foreword

I have known Rob Voorhees as a friend, co-worker in our church, and faithful parishioner for 13 years. Knowing his level of commitment and integrity alone are enough for me to get excited about this book. But when I read it for myself, I have become even more excited. I'm excited for what it has meant to me, and for what it will mean to the families who read it.

So often God's children leave too much up to God OR to Chance! For those of us who apply what we learn, this book will teach us our role in allowing God to help us achieve what he has intended for us. It will help us build a strong foundation for a great future. God will bless whatever we put our hand to, bless our **basket**, and our **store** just as He promises in Deuteronomy 28.

This book will help you map out a plan to receive the wealth that God declares is yours, and help you carry out a plan to use it wisely. If you become a doer of the godly and practical principles in these pages, your future will be what God intended it to be. "The Power to Prosper" is a God sent truth.

- Pastor Don Adkins, Family Worship Center, Lexington, Kentucky

## Eternal Gratitude

I must say it will truly take eternity to thank God for what His Son Jesus and His precious Holy Spirit have done in my life. I am a definite testimony to his promises found in Isaiah 61. I thank you Father for your undeserved love and favor that you have given to me so freely. My life's aim is to bless others the way you have blessed me. You have saved me from sin and its consequences (which are never good in the long run). You have filled me with joy and peace. You give me wisdom that mankind cannot always give, are there for me when no one else can be, and you always have the right answer at the right time for me. You have placed me in your will and I thank you in advance for such a great inheritance. Most importantly you are my very best friend who knows when I need encouragement, when I need a good talkin' to, and are wise enough to know the difference even when I disagree. I am eternally grateful. I not only owe you my life, I have given it to you because I know you do a much better job than I. I will love you with every last breath by your grace.

As in any endeavor, there is certainly more than one person that contributed to the success of this project. As many successful authors that have gone before me I want to take a moment to say thank you to the woman of my dreams.

I began praying for her at the age of fifteen, met when I was 24, she prayed for me for four years before we started dating. We have now been married for 13 years. They have been the greatest years of my life. Her continuous prodding for me to "grow up" finally has paid off. Gail, I thank God for you and will love you forever!

Any success I have is largely because of who you are. If someone were to offer me the earth for you I would tell them their appraisal is far below your market value. I know we are blessed now, but I can't wait to sit on our back porch in heaven and enjoy eternity with you.

I thank God for my children Alex and Megan whose laughter, sensitivity to God, and patience with their Daddy has always been and always will be an inspiration to me. I will love you forever and your laughter will always be some of the greatest music to which I will ever listen. Megan, you will always be my little girl from heaven and Alex, you are the best son in the world.

To my sister I say thank you for taking care of me when we were growing up so I could live long enough to learn just how great this life really is. Your love for me kept me going during times I thought I could not go any longer.

To Mom Stafford and the Stafford family I thank you for being such a wonderful example of the love of God to me. You made me a part of your family when I lost most of mine. You were the first pillar God used in building foundations in my life that only he could build. You taught me to always find a reason to praise God and always reminded me that one day I would have a family of my own. You encouraged me when I had no strength and truly healed me when I was brokenhearted. Un-describable deep joy wells up within me each time I think of you. Your reward in heaven will be great and I am grateful beyond words for who you have been to my family and me these last 30 years.

To Mom and Dad Nickel and the Nickel family I thank you for your unending love toward my family and I, your example of just how good God is, and the 20 years of memories at Thanksgiving, Christmas, and Easter. You took me into to your family like a son and just thinking about what you have done for me puts a frog in my throat. If the world was like you it would be such a better place. I can't begin to thank God enough for you.

To Pastor Don I thank you for such a wonderful example of integrity, leadership, and mercy. It is such a good feeling to have a Pastor I know I can trust and that believes in me. For the past 13 years your friendship has been a refreshing influence in my life and a great comfort in time of need. You are a true example of what a Pastor is all about. The multi racial, multi generational, multi cultural atmosphere along with the consistently positive atmosphere you and the staff deliver at our church has been an astounding testimony to what the love of God can accomplish. I have been so blessed by being with you at Family Worship Center. Your wife Mary Ann has more than once been a voice of strength for which I am grateful as well. God's blessing is upon you both and the best is yet to come as we seek him with all of our hearts!

To my many other brothers and sisters in the Lord who helped me know Him better, gain clarity in His Holy Word, and strengthened me when you did not know it, I thank God for you from the depths of my soul. I look forward to catching up with you when we get home. We'll be by the crystal clear waters of our estate listening to the waves and singing some really great heavenly songs.

# Introduction

Did you know that God himself wants to give every believer special ability to prosper? In Deuteronomy 8:18 he promises to give you "**power to get wealth**" so he can establish his covenant. That's right God wants every believer to prosper so they can in turn fund the spreading of the gospel or good news of Jesus. The bible is full of examples regarding this promise. In Genesis 15: 14 God showed Abraham the future. He told Abraham that he was going to bring his people "**out with great possessions**" from Egypt. At the time Egypt was the dominant social, cultural, military, and political force of the day. The notion that a guy with a staff and a few dollars was any match for a powerful army with an awful lot of gold was pretty silly. But we know who won that battle, Moses, the guy with the staff! When a million people or so, needed to travel through deserts hot enough to melt rubber, they were given high tech heavenly sandals to protect their feet and were supplied food from heaven while they journeyed. When Jesus needed to pay taxes, a fish suddenly appeared out of nowhere to foot the bill. When 5,000 people were very hungry the Great Heavenly Chef turned food for 50 into food for 5,000 without buying more supplies. So we can see just from these few examples that God always has and always will provide for his people. Most of the time, He blesses the work of their hands by giving them great wisdom and a spirit of excellence. At other times he bypasses the middle man and just brings the blessing miraculously. Either way, He always takes care of his kids and today is no exception. In these last days I believe the same miraculous provision we saw in these examples will take place in the near future but on a much larger scale. There is an unprecedented amount of wealth about to transfer to God's people, a Tsunami of wealth, trillions of dollars as a matter of fact. God wants his people to get prepared to receive it and teach them what to do with it so they don't squander it. **"The Power to Prosper" was written to help believers understand why God wants them to prosper, empower them to prosper, and to provide a biblical foundation for those who take the next step toward long term increase, The 10 Dimensions of Wealth Training.** The 10 Dimensions of Wealth was also created by Rob Voorhees as a personal finance training system and organizer designed to help you add "works to your faith". It combines progressive learning and the practical application of financial best practices. Be sure to take The Financial Challenge at the end of this book to discover your "financial health score".

Once you have a solid foundation of why God wants you to prosper, and how to receive it, He'll feel more comfortable turning over those "great possessions". To those who have practiced doing the right thing with their money all along, they will receive abundance. For those who know what they are going to do with it before they get it, they will be given more. Over 2000 years ago Jesus made it clear how to get more from heaven. Jesus said, "For everyone who has, more will be given, and he will have abundance; but from him who does not have, even what he has will be taken away." He made it clear that to receive from heaven you must be doing the right thing with what you already have, whether that is a $100,000.00 or $1,000.00. So to help set a solid foundation for **"The Power to Prosper"** we have created the **"10 Pillars of Prosperity".** These are little nuggets designed to get over to God's people the main reasons he wants them to prosper and some very important principles to receiving the prosperity he has promised.

**Found below are the "10 Pillars of Prosperity."**

1. The Purpose of Prosperity is to Preach the Gospel and Make Disciples of All Nations
2. For only 10% of your Proceeds and Your Promise to be Generous to others, the World's Greatest Investor will Teach You How to Prosper and Protect Your Assets
3. For Believers, There are Two Types of Prosperity, Natural and Supernatural. As in any Christian Endeavor, the Combination of the Two Breeds Success.
4. If you Take Care of Your Family God will Prosper You
5. Prosperity Begins When Your Vision of the Future Becomes Clear
6. Prosperity is the Ability to Fund What is Important to You Without Fear or Worry
7. If you don't know where your money is going, I promise you someone else does.
8. Sometimes the Question is less about Where to spend your Money than When to spend it.
9. Everyone is an Investor, they just invest in different things. For some their investments go to $0.00 within an hour. For others, their investments begin to appreciate and eventually go to work for them while they are sleeping.
10. The System of "the World" wants to Steal Your Money and Lie to You Where it Should be Spent

As you read the rest of this booklet I pray that your eyes will light up as God begins to show you your future because it can be a good one if you want it to be. I pray that you seek him with all of your heart and discover the work that you love doing. I pray that you allow God to give you special ability to do excellent work for which others will pay you a fair price and appreciate. I pray that God will give you wisdom of how to use your money without it using you. I pray especially that you remember the God who gives you the ability to get wealth and empowers you to prosper so that you can fund the very gospel that has helped you.

## *How to get the most from each pillar:*

As you read each pillar you will: 1) Have some scriptures for you to mediate upon until they become real to you. 2) You will have a suggested prayer designed to help you pray and believe God for the expected results conveyed by the pillar. 3) You will have a *"Power to Prosper Refrigerator Plan"* designed to answer where you are now, where you want to be, and how are you going to get there regarding each pillar. Copy the refrigerator plan (if you want) and place it on your refrigerator until you feel that you mastered that particular pillar. Then just repeat the process until you have completed all ten pillars.

*May the great God who teaches you to prosper guide you into all truth and set your pathway straight. May he unfold his great plan for your life and flood your very soul with a love for what you do.*

> **Prayer:** God, open the eyes of my heart that I might understand the path you have for me. Help me understand the lessons I am about to read. Empower me to prosper so I have more to give to your kingdom. In the name of Jesus I pray. Amen!

# The Power to Prosper

# Table of Contents

# Chapter 1

## To Preach the Gospel

## Pillar #1: The Purpose of Prosperity is to Preach the Gospel and Make Disciples of All Nations

It was prophesied of Jesus that he was anointed by God himself to accomplish certain things when he was here on the earth. In Isaiah 61:1 the bible says Jesus was anointed or empowered by God to preach the gospel to the poor, heal the brokenhearted, set captives free, and bring deliverance to those that were bound. In John 10:10 the bible says that Jesus came to bring us abundant life. In John 3:17 the bible says Jesus did not come to condemn the world but that the world through him might be saved. Saved from what? The world could be saved from being poor, from being brokenhearted, from feeling captive, from being bound up, and from hell which is being in an eternal state of these bad things plus eternal fire all around. It is like being in a prison in which the floor, the walls, and the bars are always on fire and will never be quenched. That's all I'm going to say about that.

One poll asked participants what they wanted more than anything in this world. The # 1 response was peace. Not world peace but personal peace. As we can see Jesus came just for that reason, to bring peace to all those mentioned in Isaiah 61:1. Everything Jesus taught was designed to bless and prosper those that were humble enough to learn from him. Of course there were those that thought they did not need him. The devil convinced them that they were either above needing him, that he would ruin their reputation, or that they would lose their constituency. Some people are like that even today.

Because Jesus came to heal all those that were oppressed of the devil and bring peace to men's souls, can there really be anything worth funding more than such an endeavor? If Jesus came to provide access to heaven on earth, can there be anything worth funding more? If Jesus brings good news in a world full of bad news, is there anything worth funding more, especially if you have been on the receiving end of any of these provisions?

When Jesus decided to implement his business continuity plan and select his successors he chose mortal men. He did not choose super heroes like Superman or Batman or Robin. He chose some fisherman, tax collectors, and other mere mortals. Why? Because Jesus had all the "super", he just needed the "man". Now today he has empowered these mere men to carry on his Father's business (Jn17). They did a great job during their time but eventually they passed the family business down to others who passed the business down to some others and on and on. Who did they pass it on to? Mere mortals you ask.. Why? Because Jesus is all the "super", he just needs man. So when it comes to solving mankind's problems there is not one single solitary better equipped problem solver than the inventor, and founder of mankind himself (GEN 1). Now there will always be those who lay claim to know more than him but we as believers just need to "eat the meat and spit out the bones" when we are forced to hear some of them. The bottom line is that if we want to make a difference in the world there is no one better equipped than Jesus. He has appointed mere men to run his business until he comes back so the gospel is preached and disciples are made through preachers and churches. I remember several years ago I had some serious back problems. I would go to work every day in pain. I had to "pop" my back 10 times a day just to help with some of the pain. One side of my ribs stood out about 2" further than the other. Part of it was from sports injuries. Part of it was because I was born with spinal meningitis and bowed legs so severe that they nearly had to break my legs to get them to grow correctly. The pain was pretty much non-stop and surgery would not help. One day my Pastor was preaching on Isaiah 53, a passage about Jesus dying on the cross for our healing. In the middle of the service I heard and felt my chest "pop" into place. My chest popped into alignment and the pain from that area has never come back since then. It has been over 15 years since that experience. Just that experience alone saved me thousands of dollars of surgery and medication. So when it comes to taking care of preachers and churches I know that it is well worth it. After 13 years of knowing my Pastor I still cannot remember anything that he has done to offend me or to set a bad example (except he did call me a mule one time when we were pouring a concrete ramp for one of our brothers in the Lord who is currently in a wheel chair. But that was because I was like the ever ready bunny bringing wheel barrow after wheel barrow of concrete up the hill). Of course you know he was just joking around. I just could not resist throwing that in here because now when he reads this book I can get him back. Deuteronomy 8:18 reminds us to "remember the Lord your God, for it is He who gives you power to get wealth, that he may establish his covenant…" His covenant is his gospel. His distribution channel is preachers. His warehouse for inventory is the local church.

It was very clear to Moses and should be very clear to us believers, that if we want God to empower us to prosper we need to remember the number one purpose of prosperity. That is so that God can establish his covenant. I once calculated how much a nice meal and premium cup of coffee costs over a period of time. If a family of four eats out twice a week at $32.50 a meal including tax and tips (a little over $8.00 each); and just one member of the family drinks a premium coffee just five days a week, that's $400.00 a month. If a twenty year old invested that money and made only 7% a year on it they would have $1,064,483.00 by the time they were 65 years old. **If I asked you to buy a $1,064,483.00 meal and a real nice cup of coffee from me, would you buy it?** Just by eating out a little less and drinking less expensive coffee just imagine how much more the gospel could go forth. I am not saying do not have fun in life, I am just saying make sure you are not wasting it when it could be put to good use.

**The #1 Pillar of the "The Power to Prosper": Remember, God will empower you to prosper when you are first focused on establishing his covenant. That is to fund local churches and preachers to preach the gospel and make disciples of all nations until he comes.**

**Prayer:** God help me to remember that there is nothing in this world more important than you and your son Jesus. Help me demonstrate that in what I say, what I do, and how I spend my money. Help me spend wisely so I have more to give to your kingdom. In Jesus Name I pray. Amen!

**Meditate on:** Isaiah 61:1, Deuteronomy 8:10 – 20, John 3:17, Genesis 1:27-30, Matthew 25:14 – 30, John 17: 1 – 23, Matthew 28: 18 – 20, Mark 16: 15

**What did you receive from these scriptures?**

**Where are you now regarding funding the gospel?**

**Where do you want to be regarding this funding?**

**How are you going to get there? (What top three actions are you going to take?)**

# Chapter 2

## How 10% Goes a Long Way

## Pillar #2: For only 10% of your Proceeds and Your Promise to be Generous to Others, the World's Greatest Investor will Teach You How to Prosper and Protect Your Assets

Many venture capital funds require 30% or more of your company in order to give you money to grow your business. Some expect 51% or more so they can have a controlling interest. The reason they want a controlling interest is because they believe they can do a better job running your business than you can. Many times they are better at it. In addition, they usually have more contacts and a broader base of expertise than you. So sometimes it can be worth it. I like to say it is better to get 49% of a $1,000,000.00 than 100% of $100,000.00. Now some of these men and woman do a really good job of growing companies. But in Isaiah 48: 17 God says he will teach you to profit and lead you in the way you should go". Most importantly he only requires a promise to be generous to others and 10% to help fund his business. He really does not even need your money but he wants to make sure you have a vested interest in the success of both his business and yours. You know, where your treasure is there will be your heart also. Now when you get down to it that is a trade just about anyone would be willing to take if they knew the whole story. I mean, think about this. With gold at $675 an ounce, a reasonable price on pearls, the going rate of communication costs, and the expected rate of alternative energy savings, the value of just five assets in heaven are worth over $1,000,000,000,000,000,000,000,000.00. That number is one nonillion. ***To put it into perspective, it would take Bill Gates over 3 million years to buy out your share of these five assets even if there were 6 billion shareholders. It would take the entire world 2500 years just to buy your share of the "business".*** And that does not include any interest! The reason I am saying this is first, I did the calculations using the most expensive alternative energy plant in the world, gates of pearl, walls of jasper, only 6" deep streets of gold and current market cap for communications companies sufficient to handle the job. Secondly God really does not need your money. One nonillion is just five of his "holdings". The rest of his assets are pretty phenomenal as well. His intellectual property portfolio of disease-curing medicine is quite enviable and he has advanced medical technology that allows individuals to live forever! So even if you made $1,000,000.00 a year, 10% would be $100,000.00 but you would have well over several quintillion in your "contract" so you would still come out pretty well.

In addition, God promises to give you your own personal body guards. They are quite impressive as well. They are undetected by the human eye, more powerful than any man on earth, and able to travel faster than light. Their only mission (and they decided to take it) is to protect and be a blessing to believers. So when God promises in Malachi 3:8 - 12 to rebuke the devourer for your sake when you bring your tithes and offerings to your church (storehouse), I think it is a pretty good investment. You could not find those types of personal protection services even if you owned half the world. Yet God provides them as part of the package when you trust him and bring your tithes and offerings to church. That is, when you bring them with a heart of gratitude and worship.

Now some of you might be struggling a little bit about the tithe. Some of you may just kind of begrudgingly throw a little bit in the plate. I am going to be a little bold here and say if you are not tithing because you love God and worship him with all of your heart, you may need to spend more time with him to realize just how good He is. The reason I say that is because it is easy to let your love for God kind of "leak out". When that happens, tithing can seem mundane. ***If tithing seems mundane it is a symptom that your relationship with God is "leaking" a little bit.*** Just look at Melchizedek and Abraham in Genesis 14: 18 – 20. This to me is the model for tithing. Here Abraham was coming home from a great victory probably just savoring the moment. All of a sudden Melchizedek appeared out of nowhere and "blessed" Abraham. As soon as Abraham received the blessing he immediately gave a "tithe" or tenth of all he had just received *in* gold, silver, and possession from his victory. As I read Hebrews 7: 1 – 4 it becomes clear that Abraham was very grateful for the blessing he received because he immediately gave him 10% of his earnings. Back then it was not part of the law. He would not have been in trouble if he did not do it. However, Abraham immediately gave 10% to Melchizedek for the blessing he received. If Abraham felt that way about Melchizedek in the Old Testament, just think what he would have done AFTER Jesus gave himself on the cross. If tithing loses its luster it is a symptom that we have a spiritual fever and need to get in God's presence until we feel better.

**The # 2 Pillar of the "The Power to Prosper": God does not require 51%. He does not require 30%. He asks you for 10%, takes all the risk of the venture, provides you with some personal body guards, teaches you how to prosper, and returns a whole lot more than what you are investing with him.**

**Prayer:** Father God, I recognize that tithing is an expression of my worship to you. I receive your promise that when I tithe in faith that you will rebuke the devil for my sake and bless me abundantly as I learn to hear your voice and do what you ask of me. Right now I receive your blessing by faith and expect you to bring the right people at the right time and the right ideas at the right time to bless me so I can be a blessing. In Jesus name I pray. Amen.

**Meditate on:** Isaiah 48:17, Malachi 3: 8-12, Genesis 14: 18 -20, Hebrews 7: 1 -4

**What did you receive from these scriptures?**

**Where are you now regarding the tithe?**

**Where do you want to be regarding the tithe?**

**How are you going to get there? (What top three actions are you going to take?)**

# Chapter 3

## The Two Types of Prosperity

### Pillar # 3: For Believers, There are Two Types of Prosperity, Natural and Supernatural. As in any Christian Endeavor the Combination of the Two Breeds Success.

Paul got kind of stern with the church at Galatia when they insisted in relying on their human abilities more than relying on God. God has made it clear that there are supernatural means of transferring wealth and he always wants us to rely on Him. If we remember the wicked servant with the two talents that did not use his money wisely, he found himself in a bad place. So there is a balance between relying solely on our humanity without trusting God at all and never doing anything because we think God is just going to do it somehow. Remember Jesus paid his taxes with heavenly assistance from a fish, Moses and his people ate manna from heaven, ravens came and fed one of God's prophets, food for less than 50 was enough for 5,000. God can supply our needs supernaturally. You might be thinking to yourself this is impossible. I certainly can understand that. But did you know it is impossible to be saved, be born again, or receive anything from God in your own ability anyway? When asked about being saved Jesus responded, "This is impossible for man but all things are possible with God." In another passage God declares it is not by might nor by power but by my Spirit says the Lord….Ephesians says you are saved by grace and that not of yourselves, it is a gift of God lest any man should boast. In another passage the word declares that "no flesh will glory in his presence." So God can and does provide supernaturally for his people. Matthew 10:27 reveals God's heart, "What I tell you in darkness, that speak ye in light: and what ye hear in the ear, that preach ye upon the housetops". Some people never take the time to hear God speak to their hearts and go out claiming to speak for him. This is a dangerous proposition. Certainly his word the bible is the final authority on every issue in life. But until it is revealed to us on the inside by the Holy Spirit we are just repeating some written words rather than sharing what has been shared with us from heaven. Deuteronomy 28: 1 declares that those who diligently listen to the voice of the Lord their God will be blessed. *1 Kings 19:12 reminds us that God speaks to us in His small still voice. If we are going to prosper beyond our own ability then we have to learn how to hear God well enough to know what to do and when to do it. If you are a Christian then, "it is given unto you to know the mysteries of the kingdom of heaven, but to them it is not given" as Matthew 13:11 prescribes. You are designed to know the will of God for your life and for your finances.*

At the same time there is a need for balance. In Paul's day there were those who were so convinced that Jesus was coming back tomorrow that they went out up on a mountain and just hung out. Now that might sound all good and well but Jesus himself said that no one knows the time or the hour that he would return except the Father. Do you remember the parable of the talents? One of the servants kind of laid down on the job and fell asleep at the wheel. The next thing he knew he found himself in hot lava with no way out. Yes God is going to bring supernatural provision to his people but he does not want us to lay down on the job waiting for it. As a matter of fact it, the provision is coming to those who are faithful to use what they already have to advance his Kingdom.

The balance is to do everything we know to, not squander our money, invest in our future, and consistently contribute to spreading the gospel. When we do what is right and learn to hear God's voice every day, He will lead us into a more prosperous life. Deuteronomy 28 starts out with, "...if you diligently obey the voice of the Lord your God...." When we get our instructions from heaven and carry them out here on earth we will prosper more.

I like to think of it like this. There are two natural laws that co exist, the law of gravity and the law of lift. Now we know that basically everything that goes up must come down. Even though that is an over simplification of the law of gravity, it works. So the notion that a plane can fly, really defies that law. So there are two laws that exist at the same time. The law of lift is greater than the law of gravity because it supersedes it. So the more momentum an object builds up the greater its chance to supersede the law of gravity. This principle is a great comparison of what I am trying to say here. You must do everything you know to do with your money that is prudent (like the law of gravity). But as the Lord directs you and you listen to him he will teach you to profit more than you could on your own (the law of lift). His ways are greater than our ways and so is his guidance when it comes to what to do with your money. Just make sure it is him guiding you anytime your financial decisions supersede plain old wisdom. In the law of lift there must be enough momentum to get off the ground otherwise you might just run into something you weren't supposed to. At the same time that you believe God for his supernatural blessing you should also put works with your faith. In James the bible says that faith without works is dead. To go up on the mountain and just hang out is to be like the unprofitable servant who found himself in a scolding hot lava bath with no way to pull the plug. No God wants us to use what we have in the way of talents gifts and abilities fervently with all of our hearts not lazily with half our hearts.

I love the story of Bezalel. You may not have heard of him. To me he represents every Christian that is not a preacher. Many Christians kind of think God only empowers his preachers. This could not be further from the truth. Now let me be the first one to say that the gospel gets preached and disciples get their start from preachers. So they are the very instrument that God chose to continue his church. But the funding for the gospel comes from the rest of the Christians and Bezalel was a perfect example how to get the job done. In Exodus 35:31 – 34 we find that the Lord "filled him with the Spirit of God, in wisdom and understanding, in knowledge and all manner of workmanship, to design artistic works, to work in gold and silver and bronze…and he put in his heart the ability to teach" Wow! God himself gave Bezalel a special ability to work in the very area he loved and gave him a special ability to teach what he loved. Now I am not sure how much better it gets than that. God wants every one of his kids to love what they are doing and give them a special ability to do it! Why? So that they can fund the gospel, make disciples of all nations, and have a lot of fun doing it in the meantime. So when it comes to combining the supernatural and the natural I cannot think of a better example than Bezalel. At least now you know who he is. *Proverbs 22:29 declares, "Do you see a man excel in his work? He will stand before kings; He will not stand before unknown men".* When you find what you love to do and excel at it, eventually you will find yourself rising to the top as you rely on God to guide you. As you rise just be sure to remember where your priorities are like Bezalel and his colleagues did. They brought their time, talents, and treasures to build the temple and God blessed them.

I have always loved having our own businesses. In fourth grade I had my first business of selling bubble gum and mazes. I would go to the general store and buy a box of gum for $5.00 and sell it to my classmates for $10.00. My mazes went from .50 - $1.50 depending on how big they were. Though my teacher shut down the business in fourth grade my love for it never waned. When I was in my twenties and mowed lawns, my clients would look at the work I did and most of the time tell me that I did not charge them enough and just voluntarily give me a bonus. When our first invention business reached a million dollar net worth, and one of our inventions grossed $3,000 a minute, it really blessed me to know how far I had come from wearing Salvation Army high-waters, food stamps, rationed showers, and just enough hot dogs and beans. But when I married the girl of my dreams I knew I truly arrived. When we watch our children grow, someone could offer me the earth and I would have to tell them I already have enough.

I read in a book one time that a very famous investor had read the bible a few times but did not understand it. Well that makes good sense because if he went to China or Mexico of Africa he would probably not understand them either. When someone else is speaking a different language you need an interpreter, unless you know the language. God's information is classified and top secret. There is not a code breaker in the universe who can break his code. Corinthians says that the natural man does not understand the things of the Spirit because they are spiritually discerned. It goes on to say, "but God has revealed them to us by his Spirit." *No human being can read the bible and truly understand it without the Great Interpreter, The Holy Spirit.* Jesus said that some people would always be learning and never come to the knowledge of the truth. This is what he was talking about. I pray for that investor that he finds the Great Interpreter, the Holy Spirit. When he receives Jesus' Spirit he will understand the bible in minutes.

Also, as you work in your current career make sure that whatever you are doing, you are doing it with all of your heart. Colossians 3:23 is pretty clear about this 'And whatever you do, do it heartily as to the Lord and not to men, knowing that from the Lord you will receive the reward of the inheritance…" Romans 12:11 reminds us to work, "not lagging in diligence, fervent in spirit, serving the Lord." Fervent in spirit indicates boiling hot or in today's words very passionate about your work. So from now on you don't have a job, you have an opportunity to worship the Lord with your work. Then you will get paid to do what you love, others will appreciate your work, and you can help fund the gospel while having fun in the meantime.

**The # 3 Pillar of "The Power to Prosper": God created you to find out what you love to do, give you special heavenly ability to do excel at it, so you can fund the gospel, and have fun doing it! You are no longer working, you are worshiping!**

**Prayer:** Father, I know that you created me for good works in Christ Jesus. I ask that you guide me in the deepest part of my soul into what I will love to do. Help me do it with all of my heart, help me do excellent work, help others to appreciate what I do, and give me a fair price so that I can help fund the gospel. In Jesus name Amen!

**Meditate on:** Deuteronomy 28: 1-15, Galatians 3: 1-5, Ephesians 2:10, John 16:13, Proverbs 22:29, Romans 12:1, Colossians 3:23, Proverbs 11:28, Matthew 10:27, 1 Kings 19:12

**What did you receive from these scriptures?**

**Where are you now regarding worshiping the Lord with your work rather than working?**

**Where do you want to be regarding worshiping the Lord with your work?**

**How are you going to get there? (What top three actions are you going to take?)**

# Chapter 4

## Funding Your Family's Future

## Pillar # 4: If you Take Care of Your Family, God will Prosper You

Proverbs 13:22 says it all, "A wise man leaves an inheritance for his children's children, and the wealth of the wicked is stored up for the righteous." If we do not look past our own generation then wealth will be short lived. This scripture shows me how God thinks. He never thinks only about today when making decisions. He also thinks how the decision today is going to affect tomorrow. Some Christians kind of think that planning for the future is wrong. If it was wrong, He would have never prophesied the coming of his Son Jesus in Genesis 3 when he told the devil that the seed of woman was going to crush his head. If planning is wrong then Hebrews would have never declared, "Jesus who the joy set before him….". If planning was wrong Jesus could have never said that in His Father's house there are many mansions. Hopefully you see my point. God knows that the decisions we make today affect tomorrow to such a degree that when Adam and Eve sinned in the garden he had already begun making plans to redeem mankind. He knew that when they sinned it would affect every single generation after them. When we make decisions today whether it is about money or anything else, it affect others. Paul said in Galatians, 6:8 "For he that soweth to his flesh shall of the flesh reap corruption; but he that soweth to the Spirit shall of the Spirit reap life everlasting." The seeds we plant today will eventually show up in the harvest of tomorrow. This includes what we say. In the ancient manuscripts of Proverbs 18:21 it becomes clear that "Death and Life are in the power of the tongue, and they that love it should eat the fruit thereof." Wisdom shows that in order to leave an inheritance to our family heirs or the next generation we are going to have to plan ahead….way ahead.

God also shows how serious he is about us taking care of our family when he says in Timothy 5:8, "But if any provide not for his own, and especially for those of his own house, he hath denied the faith, and is worse than an infidel." Now I don't know about you but I do not want that title and I certainly do not want to deny the faith! So when it comes to taking care of my family I really would rather die than to not see them blessed. Now without doubt the greatest thing I can leave my children is an example of my love for God. Proverbs 14: 26 says, "In the fear of the LORD is strong confidence: and his children shall have a place of refuge." However, I know that God wants me to provide for them financially as well. I told my wife one time that I really looked forward to getting some of things I knew she had wanted for awhile. One of them was the really nice engagement ring that was stolen from her purse. She said to me, "I know how hard you are trying honey, and I would live in a trailer in the woods if it meant being with you." Needless to say there was a frog in my throat that I did not want her to see. There is not enough money in the world to buy a wife like her! She knows that sometimes I have worked 20 hour days to get us where we want to be and her love for me inspires such work ethic. My daughter and I were just lying at the top of our carpeted stairs taking a break after an intense cleaning day at the house. She said to me, "Daddy this is the life". She was so content just being with her daddy that she had it made. She was 6 years old at the time and needless to say as I put my arm around her, gave her a big hug, and I had a frog in my throat that I hoped would go undetected. My son hurt himself playing dodge the stuffed animal one time. His head was bleeding and I brought him into the bathroom and discovered it was just a small cut. Before everything settled he said, "Daddy, I don't want to die. I want to grow up to be as good a Dad as you one day." As I hugged him needless to say there was a big frog in my throat that I was kind of hoping he could not see. God wants us to love our family and do everything we know to do to be an example for them including repent and ask forgiveness when we mess up. Not only does he want us to live out our faith in front of them but to provide for them financially. After we are on track with our tithe , our heart is to fund the gospel, we should then provide for our family. If you are not married your family is your immediate family and the family of God. How I appreciate the family of God! When I was fifteen I gave my life to Christ after my adopted mother had just passed away. She was my world at the time, and when she passed away unexpectedly while we were on vacation; my world was shaken to the core. When a fellow athlete and friend kept harassing me to read some of the tracts he was passing out, I finally read one and was struck to the core by the truth that I found in it. I lied to my friend one day when he asked me if I had given my life to the Lord the night before. I knew if I said no he would just keep preaching to me. When I lied to him and told him I had given my life to Christ, he started crying in the middle of the weight room and gave me a big hug (in front of all my macho friends). Then he said welcome into the family of God. I was struck to the core by his love for me and honestly felt Jesus right there in the weight room. However, that day I lied to him was the scariest day of my life. I truly thought the Lord would strike me with lightning for lying to one of his kids. I must have told God I was sorry 20 times that day and asked him at least that many times not to kill me. That night I did give my life to the Lord and have never been the same since. I have never found a better investment anywhere on earth. By the time two years had passed all my adopted and foster brothers and sisters had either moved out of our home because they could not stand the atmosphere or they were forced out by our adopted dad back to the state. So within the first two years I became a Christian there was no one at our house except my adopted father and I. I was very thankful for my sister Marie because she always checked in with me even though she was married at the young age of 17. To this day she is the only one out of 5 of us kids that I stay in touch with. We talk often of how much we wish we knew where our other brothers and sisters were today. We have not known the whereabouts of them for over 20 years. I am very thankful for her.

At that time, my adopted Father did not come home at night very often so I had to fend for myself when it came to cooking. Since I did not know how to cook it was not a pretty scene. I thank God to this day for the Stafford family down the street. One day I got off the school bus and Mr. Stafford said to me, "Son if you ever need a place to stay you can come live with us as long as you want." At the time I did not know what to say. I could not see my life from their vantage point. From their vantage point I was in grave danger. Looking back on it now I can see why they felt that way. Every night they invited me down to have Stafford goulash or some other wonderful tasting home cooked meal. One day I took them up on their offer to live with them. I lived with them for three years and Mom Stafford is still one of my mothers to this day. I will love them as my family forever and thank God for them eternally. If you do not have an immediate family you do have a family in the Lord.

When I moved to Kentucky to go to college I stayed in Kentucky one summer for a summer job. Through a friend the Nickel family allowed me to live with them that summer and became like a family to me. For over twenty years I have spent every Christmas, Thanksgiving and Easter at their house. They saw me through some extremely tough times in my life and they are Mom and Dad # 3. God's family is truly remarkable. ***If you don't have family you can call your own, God will find you one or two or three! Psalms 68:5 says that God is the Father of the Fatherless. I know this to be true! If you are lacking family he will find you what you need when you place your trust in him.*** Matthew 19:29 promises, "And every one that hath forsaken houses, or brethren, or sisters, or father, or mother, or wife, or children, or lands, for my name's sake, shall receive a hundredfold, and shall inherit everlasting life". I thank God all the time for this coming true in my own life. Jesus came to heal the brokenhearted, preach good news to the poor, set captives free, and free those that are bound. At one time in my life I was all of the above. He set me free. So whenever I have money, I know where it is going first! He has supplied all of my needs and I love to worship him with my giving.

So when it comes to leaving an inheritance to your children's children. God will help you along the way if to you trust him and learn to hear him. To leave an inheritance to your grandchildren or other heirs, you must learn to have your income outweigh your expenses, use your money for appreciating assets rather than depreciating ones, have adequate insurance to cover any expenses to your heirs, and fund your retirement so they do not have to. After these things are taken care of then you are on your way to leaving an inheritance to them.

If you are behind schedule just remember what Paul said in Philippians 3:13, "..forgetting those things which are behind , and reaching forth unto those things which are before." There are over 50,000 people over 100 years old in the world today. There are estimates that there will eventually be over 1,000,000 people over 100 years old in the not too distant future because of medical advancements. So if you are slightly behind schedule you may have plenty of runway to make up for lost time. I am not where I am going to be yet so I do not look behind me, I keep looking ahead!

**Pillar # 4 of "The Power to Prosper": God wants you to be a blessing to your family spiritually and financially. In order to leave an inheritance for your children's children you must have a plan for funding your own financial future so they do not have to fund it for you.**

**Prayer:** Father, I thank you for my family. I know that you bless those who take care of their family and I want to thank you for anointing me to love my family the way that you love them. Let me see them the way that you see them. Let me see them from your perspective and not just my human perspective because I recognize that your ways are much higher than my ways. So thank you for helping me love them and bless them for generations to come.

**Mediate on:** 1Timothy 5:8, Proverbs 13:22, Galatians 6:8, Proverbs 14:26, Proverbs 18:21, Matthew 19:29, Psalms 68:5, Philippians 3:13

**What did you receive from these scriptures?**

**Where are you now regarding leaving an inheritance for you heirs?**

**Where do you want to be regarding leaving an inheritance?**

**How are you going to get there? (What top three actions are you going to take?)**

# Chapter 5

## Is Your Vision Worth It?

## Pillar # 5: Prosperity Begins When Your Vision of the Future Becomes Clear

In Hebrews 12:2 the bible tells us to look "..unto Jesus who is the author and finisher of our faith, ***who for the joy set before Him*** endured the cross, despising the shame, and has sat down at the right hand of God."

What is clear to me is that Jesus did not just get thrown into a whirlwind and somehow land on the cross. Not even close! Jesus for ***the joy set before him*** went to the cross. That means that when Jesus looked out into the future and saw what he wanted to accomplish, he realized what he had to pay to get there. He had a decision to make. Is the price I have to pay worth it or not? Is the end result worth going to the cross? Resoundingly, his answer was yes! The salvation of those he loved was worth it! Personally, my life is changed because of his decision and there are millions of others who feel the same way.

***Unless your vision of the future permeates every fiber of your being then every price will be too high to get there***. I will even say this. If your vision of the future is not somehow connected to God's vision for the church in these last days (which is to preach the gospel and make disciples) then eventually you may run out of steam. That is because God already has a vision for his people. Each one of his kids know that vision deep down inside. Only as each member of the body of Christ rises up to play their role can they be fulfilled. In these last days there is an unprecedented attack of the devil to decentralize the local church. In today's world people do business with other people over the internet without ever meeting. Some very bad things have happened when predators on the internet pose as someone innocent and harmless only to cause havoc to their prey. Some Christians have stopped going to church because they feel better watching one on TV. Banks make loans to people they have never met with certain lending networks. Individuals give out information that was once taboo to total strangers. The world is quickly providing an atmosphere of "nothing local". As this unfolds, Christians will be tempted to jump on the boat and float down the river. But beware! Wolves that come in sheep's clothing have to put on their costume somewhere. If you are not part of a local church you may never see the wolf put on their costume. If you are truly involved in a local church then some of your friends and family will ask if you know the new sheep that came to church today. Eventually you and your friends will start seeing things that are suspicious for a sheep to do. Then the day will come when one of you will see the wolf putting on his costume and that person will warn all the others that indeed there is a wolf in your midst. You would never know that without being part of a local church. No church is perfect because no human being is perfect.

But Paul said in Hebrews 10:25, "Not forsaking the assembling of ourselves together, as the manner of some is; but exhorting one another: and so much the more, as ye see the day approaching". Proverbs 26: 24-26 beautifully illustrates what I am trying to say, He that hateth dissembleth with his lips, and layeth up deceit within him; When he speaketh fair, believe him not: for there are seven abominations in his heart. Whose hatred is covered by deceit, his wickedness shall be shewed before the whole congregation. ***Proverbs 18:1 says, "A man who isolates himself seeks his own desire; and rages against all wise judgement."*** In these last days it is absolutely critical to be part of a local church. If you don't like the one you are in then keep praying and searching for one until you feel a peace in the deepest part of your being. One last thing about the church, God set the model for successful churches and successful businesses in the bible. Romans 12:6-8 and 1 Corinthians 12: 3 -14 give a wonderful look into life when people with different strengths and weaknesses, different gifts and talents, decide that they can work together and become something better together than apart. We have fancy words like synergy to describe this today, but God came up with the idea first.

So your individual vision is designed to align with God's vision. *You are a piece of the puzzle and your vision is to find where you fit in the big picture not to create your own puzzle.* God's big picture begins with the local church. I love the passage in Ephesians 4:16 when Paul describes what Christian success really looks like "…from whom the whole body, being fitted and held together by what every joint supplies, according to the proper working of each individual part, causes the growth of the body for the building up of itself in love." So as a Christian there are really three primary ingredients to your vision. First it must come from God to last. Second when it comes from God it will always help the body of Christ and NEVER tear it down. Third it must reach to the deepest part of your being to where God abides, because any vision from the Lord is not done through your own might or your own power but from his Spirit helping you.

*In Proverbs 29: 18 God reminds us that where there is no vision people perish. Another translation says where there is no vision, the people are unrestrained. In both translations it is abundantly clear that unless your vision for the future is so clear and so great that you are willing to pay a price for it, then you may give up too easily and even sink into perpetual mediocrity which is like being alive but dead inside.* God has great things for your future. In Jeremiah 29:13 He promises that when you seek him you will find him when you seek him with all of your heart. We know that from Proverbs 18:9 God never blesses half heartedness or laziness. So when you sense God leading you in a direction respond wholeheartedly until he guides you otherwise. While you're at it share what you are thinking with your Pastor or one of the leaders he has chosen. They are there to help you be all that you can be in the Lord and may offer you some advice and precautions along your journey.

*I like to ask people three questions, "Where are you now? Where do you want to be? How are you going to get there?* When you decide where you want to be, it is going to have to be a noble enough cause for you to pay a price to get there. If where you want to be in the future is not clear enough or deep enough then it will end up on the shelf with many other of your good intentions. So take a moment and ask yourself what you want to leave your family when you go onto glory. What is the message you want to leave with the world? Financially speaking are you willing to sacrifice a few premium retail coffees and a few meals out to end up where you want to be? Are you willing to stay focused on the real purpose of prosperity which is to fund the gospel and make disciples of all nations? Are you willing to invest your treasures in heaven as well as your treasures on earth? Are you gearing up to leave an inheritance for your children's children?

**Pillar # 5 in The Power to Prosper: Your future begins right now, not when you arrive there! Ask God for his vision for you, how it fits into his big picture, and how to sow the right seeds in what you do and what you say to help get you there.**

**Prayer:** God I ask you to create your vision for the future inside of me. You promised that the Holy Spirit would show me things to come. So I ask you to show me enough of the future that I become passionate about the next steps I need to take. Help me see where I want to be and look forward to it every day so that the hurdles that come my way do not deter me from the good works you have for me.

**Meditate on:** John 16:13, Hebrews 12:2, Galatians 6:8, Proverbs 18:21, Ephesians 4: 16, Proverbs 29:18, Jeremiah 29:13, Proverbs 18:9, Hebrews 10:25, Proverbs 18:1, Proverbs 26:24-26, Romans 12:6-8, 1 Corinthians 12:3 – 14

**What did you receive from these scriptures?**

**Where are you now regarding your vision for the future and how it fits into God's plan?**

**Where do you want to be regarding this vision?**

**How are you going to get there? (What top three actions are you going to take?)**

# Chapter 6

## Worry Free Spending

### Pillar # 6: Prosperity is the Ability to Fund What is Important to You without Fear or Worry

I love sports. I missed Olympic trials by 15 ft in the javelin throw my senior year in high school. I also ran once in awhile. In sprinting, one of the major secrets to success is to keep your head looking straight ahead. It is disastrous to look at your opponent during the race, because where your head goes your body goes also. My senior year in wrestling I only lost to competitors that placed fourth or higher in the state. Our region was one of the tougher ones in the country. The same held true in wrestling. Control your opponents head and their body would follow. This principle is true in your finances as well. You should not look to the right or to the left to see what you neighbor is doing. You should discuss with your family what is important to you. God has a plan for you and your family that is unique and should not be compared to what another family is doing (unless your comparing which stores have the best prices). With that in mind, it is easy to talk about prosperity but it seems a little bit more difficult to define it. Some consider prosperity to occur once they have a net worth of $1,000,000.00 or more. Others consider prosperity owning a fancy car and fancy homes. In the financial industry you are called an accredited investor once your net worth reaches a million dollars or more. When one of our first businesses reached that value we felt very blessed. However, one's net worth does not mean that they have that much cash sitting around to spend. As a matter of fact, some assets might take a long time to convert into cash. Those fancy cars may not be paid for yet, and those big houses might not be paid for either. So when it comes to defining prosperity we have to take it in context. To me *prosperity is the ability to fund what is important to you without fear or worry*. Once you are tithing on all your "first fruits", your income is more than your expenses, you have 3-6 months of expenses set aside in cash, you have funded appropriate insurance policies, developed a strategy to fund your retirement, and have a strategy in place to leave something to your heirs, then you probably will have a lot less worry and fear. I know that sounds like a lot, but in order to "leave an inheritance to your children's children", these things must be done. Otherwise your children and their children will be funding you instead of you leaving something to them. But once you have a strategy in place to fund these things as God guides in his word, then you can spend your money on what is important to you as long as it does not violate God's word. As a matter of fact, Psalms 37:4 says, Delight also in the Lord and he shall give you the desires of your heart. Notice he did not say the doom, gloom, and despair of this world but the desires of your heart. 1 John 4:18 says, "There is no fear in love; but perfect love casteth out fear: because fear hath torment. He that feareth is not made perfect in love". Once you know you are on track to fulfill Proverbs 13:22 and are funding the gospel, you will feel a lot less worried, fearful, or uncertain about spending money on other things you enjoy.

**Pillar # 6 in the Power to Prosper: Once you fund the gospel and prepare properly for your family's future, you will feel much better about how you are spending your money without fear or worry.**

**Prayer:** Father, thank you for what you have given me in Christ Jesus. Compared to anything else in this world he is my greatest gift. I also know that you promised in Job 36:11 that we could spend our days in prosperity when we serve you. So I thank you by faith for the ability to hear you and serve you that I might spend my days in prosperity being blessed so I can be a blessing to others. In Jesus Name I pray. Amen.

**Meditate on:** Psalms 13:22, Psalms 37:4, Philippians 4:5-7, 1 John 4:18, Job 36:11

**What did you receive from these scriptures?**

**Where are you now regarding worry free spending?**

**Where do you want to be regarding worry free spending?**

**How are you going to get there? (What top three actions are you going to take?)**

# Chapter 7

## Who Moved Your Money

### Pillar # 7: If you don't know where your money is going, I promise you someone else does.

It is estimated that 67% of America's GDP (Gross Domestic Product) is a result of consumer spending. Basically our country is fully dependent on each one of you to spend money rather than saving it. Americans use to save 10% now they save -2%. I can't begin to tell you how many times I have talked with others about their monthly expenses and after we calculated their expenses from the top of their head and subtracted it from their income there "was supposed to be some left over money". What happens so often though is that it kind of slips away somewhere into financial limbo. The ending comment is "I'm not sure where it went". Now it is very easy to have this happen to us especially if we are not used to tracking our expenses. *However, I can tell you right now that if you do not know where your money is going someone else does.*

What I mean by that is companies spend billions of dollars every year convincing you that their product or service is the answer to your problem. Soft drink commercials are shown to quench your thirst. Health and fitness products always show the most incredible bodies and physiques to convince you that if you use their product or service that you will look like the model in TV. Snacks and candies always show someone in ecstasy as though by eating the goods you will feel like you are in heaven. Vacation commercials show families having such a great time. **What I am trying to say here is that if you don't have a plan for your money before you spend it then someone else already does.** Either through the TV, a movie, the radio or other media, companies spend billions trying to get a piece of your mind. In the marketing world it is called **"mind share"**. It means companies are trying to get you to think (with your mind) about them as an answer to a particular problem. Now don't get me wrong. Some products really do help you. I am very thankful for companies that take raw materials and make them into something we can use to support what is important to us.

*However, when those things start "pick pocketing" $10 here and the $40 there from your wallet before you have tithed, taken care of your family, funded your future, and helped others, then it might be that you have lost sight of the more important and replaced it with the immediate.*

Jesus used a parable of a sower. He said that some seeds that were sown by the sower actually started to take root but were eventually choked out by thorns and thickets. When he explained what this meant he told his disciples that this represented those who gladly received the word of God, it even took root and began to look pretty good until the plant was choked out by the cares of this life and the lust of other "things". Does God mind you having things? Absolutely not! Psalms 37:4 he is pretty clear about this when he says, "delight yourself also in the Lord and he will give you the desires of your heart. What saddens him is when those things come before the spreading of the very gospel that saved you, before your family's future, and at the expense of never helping others in need. Let not every man look only to his own affairs but also to the affairs of others it says in Romans.

The seeds you sow produce the harvest you grow. Every day you are sowing seeds in what you do and what you say. Moses said to the people right before they went into the promise land today you have the power to choose life or choose death. Then he begged them to choose life. Remember Proverbs declares that life and death are in the power of the tongue. In Galatians we see that if we sow to the flesh we will reap corruption but if we sow to the Spirit we have eternal life and peace.

**Pillar # 7 of The Power to Prosper: After you have a vision for your future that is in line with God's vision for his people, then you must aggressively protect your money to make sure it is being used to get you where you want to be. If you do not aggressively defend it, then it can easily slip right through your hands like sand.**

**Prayer:** God, help me know where my money is going before I even get it so that I can finish my race knowing that I spent my money on the vision you have for me and not on things that will not matter in the long run. Help me continuously see what lies ahead of me so I have the discipline to protect my money and spend it wisely.

**Mediate on:** Matthew 13: 3-23, Psalms 37:4

**What did you receive from these scriptures?**

**Where are you now regarding knowing where your money is going?**

**Where do you want to be regarding where your money is going?**

**How are you going to get there? (What top three actions are you going to take?)**

# Chapter 8

## When You Spend

## Pillar # 8: Sometimes the Question is less about Where to spend your Money than When to spend it.

I know some people that for some reason seem to be angry at rich folks. They kind of throw the baby out with the bathwater in thinking that every rich person uses and abuses people. I know for a fact that not ever rich person is like that. Certainly there are those who are selfish, greedy, and prideful. The same can be said about politicians. Some of them do nothing but badmouth the other party and have absolutely no desire whatsoever in helping their constituents. They enjoy the power of their position and want nothing more than to promote their party even if it means sacrificing what is right for their people. This is not a result of their money or a position; this is a result of their heart. I know many millionaires, a few billionaires, and have interviewed many other millionaires. Most of the ones I know love to help other people. I watched one of them who own tons of gas stations, entire lots of timber, high end office complexes in large cities, and thousands and thousands acres of land give away a million dollars in an hour. I know others that have built entire sports complexes for cities. Some great friends of mine who are in property management have homes worth well over a million dollars. They hire plenty of workers and create jobs. Others would give away the shoes off their feet for someone in need (I knew this firsthand as a young teenager). A Bank owner I know takes young people for rides in his Rolls Royce when they have a prom or get married. I know a business owner in the coal industry worth millions who bought his children very nice houses and loves his wife dearly. A technology owner made down payments for his children. A great minister friend of mine gave away a Lincoln Continental. Others give hundreds of thousands of dollars to their church each year.

So when I see these people riding in their Roles Royce, Mercedes, Lexus, BMWs, fancy trucks, and the like, I have no problem whatsoever rejoicing with them. I know they did not hock their future or their family to have what they have. They bought it with surplus money and they use money as a tool to spread the gospel, take care of their family, help others, and have fun. Anyone who has a problem with that scenario is probably guilty of jealousy, envy, or pride. *Abundance or the lack of it does not dictate what is in our heart. We dictate what is in our heart.*

Romans 12:15 says, "Rejoice with those who rejoice, and weep with those who weep." If you see a good person prospering and cannot rejoice with them, you ought to pray and ask God to help you rejoice with them. If they are a wicked person prospering that is a different story. For them you just need to pray that God will help them use the tool of money for good and not for evil. In these last days those who only trust in their riches will have a rough time of it eventually. If you are a child of God your inheritance is looking pretty sweet anyway. As a matter of fact, you have a share in the most expensive gated community in the history of mankind. So if you think it is wrong to have money now, God will enlighten you when you get home. *Besides, some will tell you that being rich is wrong but then come and ask you for money. I always thought this was somewhat hypocritical. If they really believed you were evil for having money or that money was evil, then why would they ask for it? Sometimes these sorts of things don't make sense.* It is almost like they are saying money is evil for you but not for us, so give it to us. If money was evil they would not have a multi-million dollar facility or even a multi – thousand dollar facility. If money was evil they would NEVER use it and live "off the land", never collect a salary, and never ask for it. Now some of those people will argue that too much money is evil. Well who then dictates how much is too much? Is $1,000 too much? Is $1,000,000.00 too much? Many of them might say anything more than what they are making is too much, because they are jealous and need to repent. I am being pretty bold here. That is because some people are spreading an awful lot of confusion and it is time to get it straightened out. The body of Christ needs to fund the gospel, take care of their families, have fun doing it, and be the example to the world God intended. *No! Money is not evil! What it is used for is either good or evil. Who would you rather have money God or the devil?*

Once in a while when I hear someone bad mouthing a CEO or a Business Owner I ask them what they would do if no one ever took the risk to start a company. Some of them understand that they would not have a job without a business owner. When I hear business owners complaining about all of their employees, I ask them what they would do if every employee in America went on strike. Then some of them remember where they came from. The truth is, if every CEO and business owner went on strike then there would not be any jobs. Likewise, if every employee went on strike there would not be enough workers to get the job done. *So like it or not owners and workers are truly dependent on each other and it is only the combination of both "gifts" that make the world what it is today. The secret is for each person to find their strengths and weaknesses, use their gift with all of their heart, and be thankful for the other gifts that make the project or company successful just like the bible describes.* Sure there is going to be some greedy selfish business owners and politicians; there will be greedy selfish employees as well. You however, will be people of passion toward your work so when you have surplus, you can buy things you enjoy.

Some people buy much more than they can afford just to look good. Their security is in what they own, what they wear, or what they drive. They buy things prematurely. When others look at them they think they are rich. In reality they are living on borrowed money and borrowed time because they cannot afford what they have. Their expenses far exceed their income. Placing trust in things that will eventually wear out is not a solid foundation. Placing your trust in the living God who said heaven and earth would pass away but His word would not pass away, is a sure foundation that cannot be moved.

Other people have worked very hard to get what they have and paid for it with surplus money after funding the gospel and taking care of their family. Those who buy prematurely before they can really afford it will find themselves in a "tight spot". Those who have surplus money should have the right to enjoy what they have worked so hard for without others ignorantly defaming them for it. There is nothing wrong with having a really nice car as long as you are not buying it with borrowed money that will jeopardize funding the gospel or your family's future. As we see in Matthew 16:26 if you have to "sell your soul" to get it then it is not time to buy it yet. Sometimes it's not what you buy but when you buy it.

Now I know that some well-known individuals preach that credit is evil. In most cases it is. But I know some individuals that have had disabling injuries, others who have outrageous medical bills, others who have lost their job and could not find work for a long time and when they did it paid much less than before. Some have had business partners betray them. There are many reasons why some find themselves in debt. Some reasons are beyond their control, some of them did not know any better, some of them knew better and should get "a whooping" from their heavenly Father. *But we cannot stereo type everyone who has been in debt. Each circumstance is different and the important thing is to look at what can be done in the future not to dwell on whether or not someone was stupid or not stupid in the past.* Just as Jesus meets us where we are to take us to where he wants us to be, the same holds true with debt and unwise financial decisions. I love the way John 3:17 puts it, "For God sent not his Son into the world to condemn the world; but that the world through him might be saved." Notice God did not send Jesus to make fun of or berate those who have sinned but to save them. The same holds true for those in debt. In some cases credit can be good. Credit is not bad when you are buying a house (as long as you can afford it) , paying for college (as long as you finish since most college graduates will make over

$500,000 more in their lifetime than those who do not graduate college), funding a business that you are competent to run, or in certain emergencies or crisis when there is no other alternative. ***Credit you cannot afford for keeping up with those who seem to have it altogether is not a good idea at all. The bible calls this presumption. Presumption is rarely a good thing.***

**Pillar # 8 in "The Power to Prosper": Sometimes it's not what you buy but when you buy it. If you have to jeopardize funding the gospel, or your family's future to buy a luxury item or discretionary item you are probably better off waiting to buy it with surplus money rather than borrowed money.**

**Prayer:** Father God I ask you to help know when to buy things I enjoy. I want to fund your good news and take care of my family first. So I rely on your wisdom to know when to buy the things I enjoy. When I buy those things, help me to keep a good attitude toward those who might be jealous or envious; because I know you have promised to bless them as well if they repent. In Jesus Name I pray. Amen.

**Mediate on:** Romans 12:15, Psalms 37:4, Matthew 16:26

**What did you receive from these scriptures?**

**Where are you now regarding when you spend your money?**

**Where do you want to be regarding when you spend your money?**

**How are you going to get there? (What top three actions are you going to take?)**

# Chapter 9

## Everyone is an Investor

**Pillar # 9: Everyone is An Investor, they just invest in different things. For some their investments go to $0.00 within an hour. For others, their investments appreciate and work for them while they are sleeping.**

As a financial and investment advisor for over six years and a business owner in one form or another since fourth grade I know that every dollar earned can either be invested in something that has a good chance of going up or a good chance of going down. I tell my family all the time to spend money on things that are going to make money or at least have a good chance of doing so. Now I am all for going out to eat. As a matter of fact, it is in our budget in the entertainment column. However, I do not know of any way to make eating out have an appreciating resale value. My wife is very frugal and I am very thankful for that. I know some women who have so many shoes that they could build a house with them. I jokingly ask them if the resale value is greater than what they paid for them. We all know the answer to that one. The same holds true with clothes. For some guys it is the car or the boat. *The question is whether or not there is a likelihood that they could sell the "asset" for more than what they paid for it. Most times the answer is no.* The same holds true for golf balls! Come on now don't yell at me just because I'm preaching good! Some people are investing in these types of things when their value goes down either within the hour or within the year. I say they are investing because for every dollar they earn they have a choice of what to do with it. No one can force us to do something with our money (unless of course it is the bill collector or the repossession company). So everyone is investing. *It is just that some investments go to zero very quickly. Is there anything inherently wrong with these things? No! There is something wrong with spending excessively when it jeopardizes funding the gospel or preparing for your family's future.* A while back I started a new budget. I say new because we wanted to cut back on our expenses while we were funding some new business ventures. I thought we had our expenses pretty "tightened up". For most people we were doing quite well.But I wanted to dig deeper. So we started a meal plan, consolidated communication costs, ate out monthly rather than weekly, refinanced our home, and found some other key areas of expense reduction. The result was that we found a way to reduce our expenses by over 20% on a monthly basis. Now we can use that money for other priorities we have. Is buying things wrong? No! If you have to sacrifice your love for God and your family's future then just repent and ask God to help you adopt his priorities for your life above your own. He promises to bless you when you do.

*On the other hand when you make wise investments that eventually go up in value and that gain interest and grow over time, your money will eventually work for you rather than you always working for it.* One of our inventions in which we invested a lot of time and money eventually received a patent, made it into national chains, and we appeared on a national television show that reached 166 million people. That particular invention averaged $3,000 a minute while with that organization. When I calculated it out it equated to $180,000.00 an hour. Even my wonderful doctor and attorney friends usually don't make that an hour. The point I am trying to make is that, when we make wise decisions with our money to invest in things that have a decent likelihood to eventually make money, it is usually better than those investments that lose value in either an hour or a week. Now whatever you do, don't just blindly invest in anything. *There is a lot to investing. I love investing. But not everyone should just arbitrarily try to invest until they have sufficient knowledge in what they are doing, or have a trustworthy advisor to guide them along the pathway.* Some suggest just throwing your money into one type of mutual fund like a growth fund. I pray they learn to be quiet in such matters until they learn the six retirement risks and at least the five fundamental retirement questions. Arbitrarily planning for such an important event as you retirement is absolute nonsense. I pray for them that the Lord will help them repent from over generalizing such important matters. As a matter of fact, we created what is called, "The 10 Dimensions of Wealth" just for that reason. It is designed to help give believers a strong foundation for some basic financial concepts to help them see "Where they are, where they want to be, and how they are going to get there practically. We designed it so that we did not have to charge the higher rates for some of our services. We felt it was one way we could "LEAVE what we have LEARNED, and are LIVING. It is one way we help others and remember that we are blessed to be a blessing.

The moral of the story here is that everyone invests because any time money comes into your hands you are choosing how to spend it. *If you spend it on things that depreciate in value, you may have a tough time reaching your financial goal of leaving an inheritance for your children's children. If you gain knowledge regarding investing, get guidance until you understand it well enough to do it on your own, and make wise decisions with your money, then eventually you will have surplus to buy whatever you like. When you do, there might be those who are quite jealous and feel you should be giving it to them instead. Just pray for them and offer to teach them what you have learned so they can apply it in their own lives. Then one more person will be blessed to be a blessing. If they don't want to listen to you then keep your blessing and just pray for them. It is possible that even if you gave them something they might squander it because they refused to learn*. Hebrews 7: 12 urges us to be imitators of those "who through faith and patience inherit the promises". **I like to say we have to be humble enough to learn from others, brave enough to apply what we have learned, and grateful enough to leave what we have learned to others.**

- Proverbs 13:20 says "He that walketh with wise *men* shall be wise: but a companion of fools shall be destroyed.
- Proverbs 13:18 declares, "Poverty and shame *shall be to* him that refuseth instruction: but he that regardeth reproof shall be honoured.
- Proverbs 10: 22 The blessing of the Lord makes one rich and he adds no sorrow..
- Proverbs 11: 26 instructs, "The people will curse him who withholds grain, but blessing will be on the head of him who sells it."
- In Proverbs 12:1 guides, "Whoever loves instruction loves knowledge but he who hates correction is stupid."
- Proverbs 18:9 proclaims, "He also that is slothful in his work is brother to him that is a great waster."
- Proverbs 12:9 reminds us, "He that is despised, and hath a servant, is better than he that honoureth himself, and lacketh bread."
- Proverbs 12:24 warns, "The hand of the diligent shall bear rule: but the slothful shall be under tribute."
- Proverbs 15:32 prods, "He that refuseth instruction despiseth his own soul: but he that heareth reproof getteth understanding."
- Proverbs 20:4 cautions, "The sluggard will not plow by reason of the cold; therefore shall he beg in harvest, and have nothing."
- Proverbs 25:12 determines, "As an earring of gold, and an ornament of fine gold, so is a wise reprover upon an obedient ear."

You might ask why I included all of these scriptures. That is because you need to get a good understanding on how to make your money grow in value and work for you when you are asleep. Use the money that you earn from the special abilities that God gives you and invest it wisely so that it will grow in value rather than going to zero in seconds. Throughout all of my careers with Fortune 10, Fortune 50, and Fortune 300 companies I always asked a lot of questions. One time when I was in a high level management meeting they nicknamed me "sponge".

That is because I spent as much time as I could learning from the best in the field so I could emulate their success. I interviewed hundreds of successful people and did everything they taught me to the best of my ability.

**In the ancient manuscript of Proverbs 25:2 we find, "It is the glory of God to conceal a thing: but the honour of kings is to search out a matter."**

*If you want to learn something from God you are going to have to search it out. He blesses diligence not laziness. He blesses those who have a heart to learn not a heart to be complacent. He cannot bless those who enjoy mediocrity. Become a "sponge" until you can stand on your feet. The only ones who will fault you for that are those who will eventually watch you pass them by.*

**Pillar # 9 in "The Power to Prosper": Everyone is an Investor. It's just that some people invest in things that depreciate in seconds and others do not.**

**Prayer:** Father help me to learn to invest in those things that have a good likelihood of going up in value rather than those things that go down in value quickly. I want to learn from you and I ask you to guide me to those who can help me learn until I have learned enough to invest on my own. I love learning and want to have my money work for me not the other way around. You promised if I seek you I would find you and I seek you with all of my heart in this matter. In Jesus name I pray. Amen!

**Mediate on:** Hebrews 7: 12, Proverbs 13:20, Proverbs 13:18, Proverbs 10: 22, Proverbs 11: 26, Proverbs 12:1, Proverbs 18:9, Proverbs 12:9, Proverbs 12:24, Proverbs 15:32, Proverbs 20:4, Proverbs 25:12, Proverbs 25:2

**What did you receive from these scriptures?**

**Where are you now regarding investing your money?**

**Where do you want to be regarding investing your money?**

**How are you going to get there? (What top three actions are you going to take?)**

# Chapter 10

## The Thief Can be Caught You Know

### Pillar # 10: The System of "the World" Wants to Steal Your Money and Lie to You Where it Should be Spent

We know that in John 10 "The thief has not come but to kill steal and destroy…" *Sometimes however he is interested in stealing a penny at a time more than he is stealing a lot of your money at once. He knows that if he tried to steal $100,000.00 from the average American family they would become very upset and probably even fight back. But if he can steal $10.00 here and $40.00 there then it could be virtually undetected for an average family in America.*

If the top priority of God is to preach the gospel to all the earth and make disciples of all nations then we know that the number one goal of the devil is to stop that from happening. So when it comes to your money, the devil has all kinds of uses for it. Mainly he wants you to spend your money on things that depreciate in value, do not spread the gospel, and are long term bad for your family.

I saw an article several years ago called the cashless society. It was an article written about the credit card industry. One of the industry leaders was quoted as both wanting and predicting a cashless society. The reason they wanted a cashless society was because they knew that most everyone with a credit card would pay them interest. Interest on one billion people with $1,000 balance adds up quickly. As a matter of fact, that works out to be $100,000,000,000.00 a year in interest. That is one hundred billion dollars in interest each year. Now you can see why credit card companies and some other lenders want your money so badly. They make their presence in your life so small that they are virtually undetected. I'm talking of course about that very small piece of plastic in your wallet called a credit card.

**Pillar # 10 in "The Power to Prosper": Jesus said that his sheep would hear him and not listen to a stranger. This promise is just as real when it comes to your money as in any other area of life. The stranger is the world's system trying to convince you how to spend your money. God wants to guide you how to spend your money so it will help you be fulfilled as a Christian by spreading the gospel, take care of you in later years, help you leave something for your heirs, and bless you with the desires of your heart.**

**Prayer:** God please help me to hear your voice when it comes to money. You promised me that if I lack wisdom I can ask you for it and you would give it to me according to James 1. So I ask you now for your wisdom regarding my money. I submit myself to you and resist the devil's plans for my money therefore he must flee. In Jesus name I pray. Amen

**Mediate on:** John 10:4-5, James 4:7, John 10:10, Proverbs 3:5-6

**What did you receive from these scriptures?**

**Where are you now regarding someone stealing your money?**

**Where do you want to be regarding someone stealing your money?**

**How are you going to get there? (What top three actions are you going to take?)**

# Chapter 11

## Take the Challenge

Before we say goodbye, I would like you to take a moment and join me in a challenge. I call it The Financial Challenge. I truly believe that Christians are going to have an unprecedented opportunity to utilize significant wealth in the near future. However, I believe that those who can hear the Lord sufficiently enough to carry out his will and combine financial best practices will be the most effective with it. We designed the challenge to help believers evaluate where they truly are financially. It is the next step towards your financial success. ***If I could beg you to take it I would.*** If you get an "A" on it you may not need the training. If you get less than an "A" then I challenge you to "increase learning" as Proverbs 1:5 urges. So without further adieu please take three minutes to complete the Financial Challenge.

## HOW IS YOUR FINANCIAL HEALTH DOING?

When was the last time you had a checkup? We invite you to take the financial health challenge so you can discover your FINANCIAL HEALTH SCORE. Honestly answer the following 12 issues.   For each issue for which you answer **yes, assign a value of 8** in the score column. When you are finished answering the questions then total your score.

| | **Financial Health Issue** | Yes | No | Score |
|---|---|---|---|---|
| 1 | My budget is based on my long term financial goals, is reasonable, and is measurable. | | | |
| 2 | I know my credit score and understand its importance to my overall financial health. | | | |
| 3 | I know my current net worth and have a plan to increase it. | | | |
| 4 | I have calculated how much insurance I need and what types best fit with my situation. | | | |
| 5 | I have addressed the five primary retirement questions and the six retirement risks. | | | |
| 6 | I know what company stock options are available to me and if they make sense. | | | |
| 7 | I know the 10 basic concepts of investing and have applied them to my investment strategy. | | | |
| 8 | I know the four basic stages of a business cycle, the 7 steps of business succession planning, and have adequately addressed these issues. | | | |
| 9 | I know the options in titling my assets such as my 401K, 403b, my primary residence, my automobiles, and have titled them properly. | | | |
| 10 | I understand the term Durable Power of Attorney, have selected one, and have also considered successors. | | | |
| 11 | I understand the difference between an Executor and a Trustee, have selected one, and have also considered successors. | | | |
| 12 | I know the four stages of wealth management and have adequately prepared for the final two stages. | | | |
| | Score Total | | | |

Scoring: A - (82 – 96), B- (76-81), C- (68-75), D- (60-67), E- 60 or below

### HOW DID YOU DO?

**If you are *below* an "A"** then consider taking **"10 Dimensions of Wealth"** Training to increase your financial health. The training will equip you with the financial tools you need to confidently answer the 12 Financial Health Issues found above. To find out more visit our website at www.financialeadership.com  OR email us at rob@voorheesco.win.net  and request information for "The 10 Dimensions of Wealth".

# Chapter 12

## Parting is Such Sweet Sorrow

### Summary

God is going to pour out prosperity in an unprecedented fashion to his people in these last days. It will make the possessions that Israel took out of the land of Egypt look small. My prayer is that you are ready for it when it comes; that you begin to look out into the future and use your money wisely to fund the gospel, protect your family's future, and have fun doing it. I pray you have been encouraged and inspired in knowing that God himself wants to give you "Power to Prosper". It might be as when Jesus had a fish pay his tax bill for him. Most of the time it will be like Bezalel, when God filled him with the Spirit to do great work, love what he was doing, and have fun doing it. If your heart is to fund his gospel, take care of your family's future, be a blessing to others, work with all of your heart, and to have fun doing it, then your future is bound to get better than it already is. As you learn the 10 Pillars of "The Power to Prosper" and apply them to your own circumstances, I pray that you remember to leave what you have learned to others so they can be blessed as well. If you are a believer you are part of his family, and his family not only has a great inheritance coming in the hereafter, it has a great inheritance coming while we are in earth. Soon his glorious good news will be preached to all nations, his people will mature into the greatness he has always intended, and at just the right time we will all meet together for a huge feast and a great party. We'll be in the most incredible gated community in the history of mankind. There will be no more sadness or sorrow. The temperature is going to be perfect. The food is going to be delectable. There will be "nothing but love"! There will be no more evil to worry about. Best of all we will be with those we love the most and that includes the King of Kings Himself our Lord Jesus! If I don't see you here I'll meet you at the family reunion! In the meantime, I look forward to prospering with you and being a blessing to others.

May God's best be yours in unprecedented ways,


Brother Rob Voorhees

Email us at: rob@voorheesco.win.net  to request additional copies

www.ingramcontent.com/pod-product-compliance
Lightning Source LLC
Chambersburg PA
CBHW041236040426
42445CB00004B/48